Ingredients

Base:

- Family
- A handful of friends.
- Lots of activity.
- A strong dose of values.
- Enough sleep.

Filling:

- 500 grams of positive thinking.
- 3 tablespoons of fun.
- 1 cup of laughter.
- A dash of “me time”.
- A touch of humour.
- A pinch of stress.

Topping:

- A sprinkle of smiles.
- A dollop of sunshine.

Method

Base:

1. Combine family and some good friends. This will form a strong base.

Cook's tip:
Allow plenty of time for friendship bonds to strengthen.

2. Add lots of exercise to the mix. Stir well!

Cook's tip:
Being active is good for the body and mind.

3. Pour a strong dose of values into the mixture. Allow this to sit.

Cook's tip:
Values help you to live your life in a meaningful way. Ingredients such as being honest and caring for others would spice up this dish.

4. Allow mixture to rest overnight so that base becomes firm.

Cook's tip:
Get enough sleep each night. This is important for a healthy body and mind.

Filling:
5. Mix helpful thoughts and positive thinking. Stir well.

Cook's tip:
Counting your blessings can improve your wellbeing.

6. Add three tablespoons of fun. Add half a cup of laughter and your sense of humour.

Cook's tip:
If the filling feels too tight, laughter can loosen it up.

7. Remove negative self-talk with a sifter.

Cook's tip:
Negative self-talk can prevent your cake from rising. Try positive self-talk – it acts like self-raising flour.

8. Scoop filling into a pot and add a pinch of stress. Simmer on the stove but do not let contents boil over.

Cook's tip:
A little stress is normal. This can add to the flavour. Too much stress can spoil the dish.

9. Spread filling evenly over the base and bake in the oven. While waiting, relax and have some "me time".

Cook's tip:
Take a few minutes to sit back and do nothing. This can be a great way to de-stress.

10. Sit back, breathe deeply and smell your creation as it cooks.

Cook's tip:
Take notice of the present. This can help stop you dwelling on past cooking mistakes.

Topping:

11. Remove cake from oven and top with an extra 3-4 assorted friends.

Cook's tip:
You can never have too many friends.

12. Drizzle the remaining half cup of laughter over your creation. Now sprinkle with some smiles. Finish with a dollop of sunshine.

Cook's tip:
Caution: Laughter and smiles can spread quickly.

13. Accept that your cake won't be perfect. Focus on what you did well. Learn from your mistakes.

Cook's tip:
Accept who you are. Don't wish you were someone else. You may never be the world's best chef. You can try, however, to improve your cooking. Focus on your strengths and not your weaknesses.

14. Eat your cake but share it with others too. Now learn a new recipe.

Cook's tip:
Giving to others and being kind helps other people. Being kind also makes you feel good. Learning a new skill helps keep your brain fit.

15. Repeat steps 1-14 for the rest of your life.

Cook's tip:
Your mind is like your body – you have to take care of it.

Activities

Talk about what these images are telling you about the story.

Activities

Talk about what these images are telling you about the story.

Activities

Talk about what these images are telling you about the story.

Activities

Talk about what these images are telling you about the story.